Sheetala puja

Bengali Puja Padhyati

Contributions: Aparna Sen Naskar
Purwa Chakraborty

Publisher: DivineBharat

Sheetala Puja

Bengali Puja Padhyati

Contributions: Aparna Sen Naskar
Purwa Chakraborty

Publisher: DivineBharat

ISBN:978-93-5655-264-7
Email: info@divinebharat.com
Website: www.divinebharat.co

Index

Introduction

Sheetala Maa is a highly revered goddess in the rural and folk religious traditions of Bengal. She is primarily worshipped as the destroyer of diseases, the bestower of cooling relief, and the embodiment of gentle, soothing divine power. It is believed that Goddess Sheetala protects devotees from fever, heat rashes, measles, chickenpox, smallpox, skin diseases, and various infections affecting children. For this reason, her worship is still performed with great devotion in households across Bengal, especially in rural areas.

The word *"Sheetala"* is derived from *"sheet"* or *"coolness."* Goddess Sheetala represents the calm and cooling energy that removes bodily and mental heat, illness, impurity, and restlessness, and grants peace, serenity, and good health.

She is usually depicted as:
• Riding on a donkey,
• Holding a broom, symbolizing the sweeping away of disease and impurity,
• Holding a water pot (kalash), symbolizing purity and the flow of life,
• Holding neem leaves, which are known in Ayurveda as powerful disease-healing and cooling agents.

A special feature of Sheetala Puja is that it is a **fireless ritual**. On the morning of the puja, no cooking is done. It is believed that fire and heat are contrary to the calm and cooling nature of the goddess. Therefore, all offerings, food, and prasad are prepared on the previous day and offered as leftover food (*bashi anna*).

The worship of Sheetala Maa is generally performed:

- At home with family members,
- In village temples, or
- According to special rituals dedicated to Sheetala Thakurani puja.

Although the puja is observed on different dates in different regions, it is almost everywhere performed before dawn, when the air is comparatively cool and the surroundings are calm and pure—conditions that align with the cooling nature of the goddess.

Through this worship, devotees pray for the well-being of the family, the health and long life of children, protection from diseases, social harmony, and happiness and prosperity in household life.

Scriptures and devotional traditions dedicated to Goddess Sheetala include:

- Sheetala Dhyana Mantra,
- Aavahan Mantra,
- Sheetalashtakam,
- Sheetala Stotra,
- Sheetala Kavacham,
- Sheetala Chalisa.

It is believed that reciting these purifies both the mind and the surrounding environment.

Sheetala Puja has deep roots in folk culture, Ayurveda, rural healing traditions, and the worship of the divine mother. The goddess is revered as *"Maa"*—a mother who does not allow her children to suffer from fever, protects them from illness, and removes unrest from the household, establishing peace and harmony.

Through Sheetala Puja, devotees pray for:

- Freedom from disease,
- Peace of mind,
- Good health and long life for the family,
- Relief from sorrow and suffering,
- Prosperity and protection of the home.

Sheetala Puja

Complete Ritual Procedure

Required Materials

---

1. One small idol or picture of Goddess Sheetala Maa
2. Kalash (filled with water) — decorated with water and neem leaves
3. Marjani (broom) — for symbolic use
4. Kalash / lota / small sprinkler
5. Neem leaves, tulsi leaves (if available), arata leaves
6. Flowers — white or light-colored flowers are preferred
7. Incense (optional) — traditionally Sheetala Puja is fireless, so it is better to avoid incense that requires fire
8. Cooling items: cool water, milk, jaggery, khichuri / leftover rice, salt, curd — for prasad
9. Aarti plate (without using a lamp). Aarti may also be done using a mirror, chamor, or flowers

10. Rangoli or clean cloth, bowls for keeping prasad
11. Handkerchief, bell — optional
12. Written sankalp (on paper or phone)

Pre-Puja Preparations

---

1. Purity: Clean the house and the altar. Wash hands and face, and wear clean clothes.
2. Altar Arrangement: Place the idol/ picture on the altar. Arrange the kalash, marjani, neem leaves, flowers, and prasad nearby.
3. Food Rules: On the morning of the puja, no fresh cooking should be done.
   - Prasad should consist of leftover rice from the previous day, payesh, fruits, jaggery, and dry fruits.
4. If the puja is performed in a group: Select one person to act as the karta (chief worshipper).

Puja Sequence (Main Section)

1) Dhyana (Meditation and Mental Preparation)

Sit calmly and steady the mind for 1–2 minutes, focusing on peace.

Chant:

Om Sheetalaang Devim
Dhyaayami
Rasabhasthaang Digambareem
Marjani Kalashopetaang
Surpaalankrita Mastakam

(Meditate on Sheetala Maa in her donkey-mounted form.)

2) Sankalpa (Statement of Intention)

State your name, place, and purpose of the worship.

Om Shaantih Shaantih Shaantih
Aham (your name**) Sheetala**
Poojaang Karishyaami
Mama Parivaarasya Mangalarthe
Roga Naashaarthe
Suswasthya Laabhaarthe Karomi

3) Achaman / Shuddhi
(Purification)
Wash your hands and chant "Om Shaantih" three times.
Take three drops of water as achaman.
Offer pranam with folded hands to the altar and the surroundings.

4) Aavahan (Invocation of the Goddess)
Facing the idol or kalash, chant:
Om Shri Sheetala Devyai Namah

5) Nyasa (Optional)
Touch the forehead chanting **"Om Hreem",**
Touch the heart chanting **"Om Hoom".**
Touch the kalash three times while performing nyasa.

6) Dhyan Mantra

Om Sheetalaana Devata Lakshmi
Beejam Bhavani Shaktih
Sarvabisphotaka Nivrityarthe
Jape Vyavahritah

Dhyan Mantra
Om Sheetala Shobhana Shubhra
Shubhda Shobhanaprada
Shubhda Shobha Shubhayuta
Shishu Byadhi Vinashini

Shishudatri Shishubhrita
Shishu Dukha Vimochini
Shishudya Shishugha Shubhra
Shuddha Shuddharaktabashini

Shivapriya Shashimukhi
Shubhrangi Shubhabhushana
Shukrada Shushkaha Shweta
Shweta Byadhi Vinashini

Shwetambara Shwetohara
Shwetadwipa Nivasini
Shwetopabasana Chaiva
Shwetapadma Vibhushana

Shankari Shantida Shanta
Shantishankara Priya
Shokanasha Shokahara
Shokada Shokanashini

7) Stotrapath / Japa (Main Ritual)

At this time, recite the complete **Shri Sheetala Devi Stotra, Sheetalashtakam, or Sheetala Kabacham.**

If you are unable to do so, perform a simple japa instead—

Om Sheetalayai Namah (108 times) or **Om Shri Sheetala Devyai** Namah (108 times)

Prarambha Shloka

Om Sheetala Shobhana Shubhra
Shubhda Shobhanaprada
Shubhda Shobha Shubhayuta
Shishu Byadhi Vinashini

Shishudatri Shishubhrita
Shishu Dukha Vimochini
Shishudya Shishugha Shubhra
Shuddha Shuddharaktabashini

Shivapriya Shashimukhi
Shubhrangi Shubhabhushana
Shukrada Shushkaha Shweta
Shweta Byadhi Vinashini

Shwetambara Shwetohara
Shwetadwipa Nivasini
Shwetopabasana Chaiva
Shwetapadma Vibhushana

Sheetala Stotra (Bengali)

1

Namah Shwetabasanadharini
Shashimukhi Shantidayini
Nimpatrashone Biraj
Jwararupa Peera Harini

2

Dhenuki Bahini Devi
Bhaktashoka Binashini
Marjanihaste Janani
Gramraksha Karunamoyi

3

Shishur Byadhi Nash Koro
Ghorghore Mongol Dao
Ashanti Dur Koro Maye
Tomar Name Japa Gao

4

Shubhra Dibya Sharirdharini
Karunasindhu Janamoni
Je Toke Sharan Ney Ma
Tar Abhoy Tumi Dan Koro

5

Rajarog Peera Nashini
Dushanti Dahoni Devi
Sheetalarupe Tumi Ma
Shanti Alo Borshao Niti

6

Matah Taba Padapadme
Amar Sharan Sthir Hok
Taba Kripay Deha Mon
Pak Shantir Param Lok

7

Joy Joy Sheetala Mata
Bhuban Raksha Koro Sada
Bhaktadukkho Dur Koro Ma
Charone Roi Shir Nata

Iti Sheetala Stotram

Sheetalashtakam

Om Gardabharudha Chhinna
Bheshaja Bhava Padmavasini.
Kritva Kaksham Rakshyet
Baksham Dakshine ShubhaMarjani.
Byadhivatsa Pretangsha
Prajabuddhi Karini.
Hreem Namami Sheetale
Sankate Ghoratarini 1

Nam Shabda Jiba Japet
Jambudwipa Vasini.
Tejogarbha Mahakharpa
Jibadarpa Harini.
Shyamabarna Ghatakarna
Sthiraraja Grihini.
Hreem Namami Sheetale
Sankate Ghoratarini 2

Briddhakesha Pankakesha
Haste Yantradharini.

Kumudababadana Bhale
Bindu Teja Bindu Karini.
Anadrishta Indusadrisha
Asatyarupa Dharini.
Hreem Namami Sheetale
Sankate Ghoratarini 3

Jwarakrantajna Matra
Shasitatro Medini.
Bhumikampa Mahadagdha
Dushtadanta Karini.
Tejomayi Sarvajayi
Brahmamayi Namami.
Hreem Namami Sheetale
Sankate Ghoratarini 4

Bisphoranaduki Purnamurti
Byadhikashta Karini.
Tanmata Jagatkhyata
Jagatprana Dayini.
Yogamarga Bhoga
Tinabarga Tushtada.

Hreem Namami Sheetale
Sankate Ghoratarini 5

Jagaddhatri Purnamurti
Adyashakti Dharini.
Janmato Jagatkhyata
Jagatprana Dayini.
Dushtahantri Tripurabhi
Manohari Mohini.
Hreem Namami Sheetale
Sankate Ghoratarini 6

Suprakashi Dasadasi
Ashtahasi Badaki.
Range Bhange Byadhisange
Raktabati Sangini.
Shabdamatre Sarvashranta
Lomashru Karini.
Hreem Namami Sheetale
Sankate Ghoratarini 7

Nijadase Suprakase
Prasanna Ma Brahmani.
Brahmagyan Tapadhyan
Sarvatra Traskarini.
Tanmantra Gyanamastre
Charanapadya Dayini.
Hreem Namami Sheetale
Sankate Ghoratarini 8

Brahmayamale Brahma Narada
Sambade Sheetalashtakam.

Shri Sheetala Sahasranam (Namavali – Prarambha)

Shantipriya Tu Shantimayi
Shantimada Priya Tatha,
Shwetamalyapriya Shighra
Shighrada Shighraha Shiva.

Shayya Shayana Shyamangi
Shyama Shyamabimohini,

Shayakishi Shabarudha
Shmashanalayavasini.

Shadbhuj a Shadras a Chaiva
Shadrasaralolupa,
Shanmukhi Shaddalayuta
Shadrasarajanani Tatha.

Sati Satyapriya Chaiva
Satyapalanatatpara,
Satya Satyavati Chaiva
Sarvadanavaghatini.

Sarvani Sarvarupa Cha
Sarvabhagyapradayini,
Sarvaishwaryayuta Chaiva
Sarvaishwaryapradayini.

Sarvadatri Sarvagrahi
Sarvapalanatatpara,
Saubhagyadayini Chaiva
Sarvadukhabinashini.

Sarvasampatpradatri Cha
Sarvasukhadayini,
Sumukhi Sarvajanani
Sarvadhara Sadasthira.

Hara Haimavati Homadatri
Harabilasini,
Harapriya Harananda
Haradukhavimochini.

Shri Sheetala Sahasranam (Mula Path)

Harinamapriya Chaiva
Harinamaparayana
Harinamaratashchaiva
Harinamarata Sada

Harinamaprítichaiva
Harinamaparayana
Harinamaratastu Chaiva
Harinamapradayini

Haripriya Haripuja
Haripad anukulini
Haripada Padmasanglagna
Haribhaktipradayini

Harilila Harishakti
Haribratarata Shubha
Haripujanatatpara
Harinamarchanashrita
Harinamaratashchaiva
Harinamasutopama
Harinamastutichaiva
Harinamapradayini

Harinamasadananda
Harinamarata Sati
Harinamapriya Chaiva
Harinamabibardhini

Harinamapradatri Cha
Harinamapalika Tatha

Harinamaratashchaiva
Harinamaparayana

Kastanashini Prasanga

Kastada Kastaharini
Kastanashini Cha Sa
Kastaha Kastadatri Cha
Kastapeeranibarini

Kamaprada Sheetala Devi

Kamada Kampalika Cha
Kamarupa Shubhaprada
Kamini Kamahartri Cha
Kamadatri Cha Kamini

Kamaprada Kamasukhada
Kamakelipriyanchita
Kamanashini Cha Devi
Kamadatri Manohara

Kamapeeraharachaiva
Kamaha Kamadayini
Kamarata Kamabija

Kamarupa Shubhanana

Kamada Kamaha Chaiva
Kamadatri Manohara
Kamasangharini Devi
Kamapeeranibarini

Kamarata Kamasukhada
Kamarupa Shubhanana
Kamaprada Kamada Chaiva
Kamadatri Manohara

Shuddharupa Sheetala

Shuddha Shuddhabrata Chaiva
Shuddhasattva Manohara
Shuddhacharapriya Chaiva
Shuddhapranapradayini

Shuddharupa Shuddhabuddhi
Shuddhakarmarata Shubha
Shuddhabhaktiprada Chaiva
Shuddhapriya Shubhanana

Shuddhasattva Shuddhagati
Shuddhabuddhipradayini
Shuddharata Shuddhachita
Shuddhacharaparayana

Shuddhasangya Shuddhadrishti
Shuddhahasyavibhushita
Shuddhagatra Shuddhabakya
Shuddharupa Manohara

Shuddhanana Shuddhabuddhi
Shuddhakirti Shuchismita
Shuddhacheta Shuddhamati
Shuddhapadapranamini

Bishphotakanashini Sheetala

Bishphotakanashini Devi
Bishphotakabhayapaha
Bishphotakapeerahaarini
Bishphotakanibarini

Bishphotakapeerahaarini
Bishphotakapradahini
Bishphotakabinashini
Bishphotakanashini

Bishphotakabinashini
Bishphotakabhayapaha
Bishphotakapeerahaarini
Bishphotakanibarini

Bishphotakasangharini
Bishphotakamahaarini
Bishphotakamaharajni
Bishphotakabinashini

Jwararoga Prashamani

Jwararogaprashamani
Sheetalapriya Sarvada
Jwararoganashini Devi
Sheetalangana Sundari

Sheetalalingita Devi

Sheetalangapradayini
Sheetalapranadatri Cha
Sheetalalokabardhini

Sheetalanukampita Devi
Sheetalanandabardhini
Sheetalapritida Devi
Sheetalanandadayini

Sheetaladarshanasukhada
Sheetalapremabardhini
Sheetalanamagana Priya
Sheetalapujanatushtida

Sheetalashrayini Devi
Sheetalabhaktimanasa
Sheetalapprananilaya
Sheetalapadasannata

Samapani Shloka

Iti Shri Sheetala Sahasranam
Sampurnam
Om Tat Sat

Atha Sheetala Kabacham

Devi Uvacha

Om Bhagavan Bhutabhavesha
Pradhanapurusheshwara.
Tvatprasadat Vijnatam
Sarvachara Charotkritam.
Agameshu Cha Sarveshu
Mantra Mantra Yathoditah.
Idanim Shrotum Ichchhami
Kabacham Roganashanam.

Devyah Shri Sheetalayashcha
Kabacham Na Prakashitam.
Tanme Kathaya Devesha
Yadyanugraho Hasi Me.

Shri Mahadeva Uvacha

Sadhu Sadhu Mahabhagye
Jagatanam Hitakarini.
Pravakshyami Visheshena

Kabacham Paradurlabham.
Yajnatva Munayah Sarve
Rogashoka Vivarjitah.
Devashcha Danavah Sarve
Gandharvah Kimnarastatha.
Naga Manushyashcha Yeke Chit
Sarve Rogavivarjitah.

Pranabo Me Shirah Patu
Bhalam Shri Sheetala Tatha.

Nasikang Bahanijaya Cha
Mukham Ashtanga Karo Manuh.

Jihvayang Bagbhavam Bijam
Chakshuh Kamabija Karmani.

Mayabijam Tu Karnau Me
Kanthadesham Kalika.
Skandhau Devi Sada Patu
Roganam Janani Mama.

Bahu Kakshau Tatha Bakshah
Stanodara Katimarma.
Satatam Patu Mam Devi
Sarvaroga Binashini.

Guhyam Lingam Tatham eshru
Yugang Tathaiva Cha.
Padau Dau Patu Mam Nityam
Sada Gadabibahini.

Rakshashilandeshu Yatsthanam
Barjitam Kabachena Tu.
Tat Sarvam Raksha Devi
Mahavidya Dashakshari.

Evam Nyasabidhim Kritva
Japet Mantram Manankshi.
Pranabam Purvam Uccharya
Bagbhavam Tadanantaram.

Kamabijam Tatah Pashchat
Mayabijam Tadanantaram.

De Yuta Sheetala Cheti
Bahnijaya Samanvita.

Dashakshari Mahavidya
Sarvasampatkari Shubha.
Vidyashtakshari Devi
Kamamaya Bibarjita.

Mantroddharam Imam Bhakte
Snehadaham Guhogopitah.
Maharogopashantyartham
Japet Ashta Sahasrakam.

Japo Homa Purashcharya
Mantranam Ayuta Japesh Sah.

Sheetala Purvadigbhage
Archyey Roganashini.
Dakshine Dakshinakali
Mundamala Bidarini.

Nairityang Patu Mam Nityam

Suryalankrita Mastaka.
Pashchime Patu Mam Nityam
Shubha Marjjani Kara Tatha.

Bayabyang Patu Mam Devi
Sada Kaler Dharini.
Digambari Sada Patu
Uttarasyang Sanatani.

Aishanyang Dishi Mam Patu
Satatam Ghoradarshini.
Urdhvadah Kramato Rakshatu
Sheetala Sheetalaprada.
Rajadware Shmashane Cha
Rogodbhute Tatha Pathe.
Sarvato Patu Mam Nityam
Sheetala Surpadharini.

Iti Te Kathitam Devi
Kabacham Roganashanam.
Na Yasmai Kasmai Na Databyam
Yadicched Atmano Hitam.

Puja Bidhaya Mahatim
Gurum Abhyarchya Sadhakah.
Ashtottarashatam Bapi
Sahasram Ba Bisheshatah.

Roganam Hrasabriddhing
Gyatwa Japet Shubham Labhet.
Bhaktiyuktaya Shantaya
Sadhakaya Dwijaya Cha.

Sada Deyam Na Deyam
Dattikaya Shathaya Cha.
Stribhaya Dharmahinaaya
Paradararataya Cha.

Bidweshakaya Dushtaya
Jibarnamahitacharane.
Ghore Bishphotake Chaiva
Mahabyadhi Samupasthite.

Galagandaadi Rogeshu

Pathitabyam Sadabudhaih.

Idam Kabacham Agyatwa
Yah Kuryach Sheetalarccanam.
Sah Hinayu Nirdhanah Papi
Byadhibhih Paripiritah.

Putradibhih Sarddham Labhet
Yama Yatana.

Chetasa Bhaktiyuktena
Pujayitva Digambarim.
Yah Pathet Kabacham Devi
Sah Sheetala Phalam Apnuyat.
Bisheshatah Kalou Devi
Kalidukkha Bimochini.
Sheetalang Pujayed Vidwan
Mahabipad Imabrishu.

Kritva Tu Pratimang Dibya
Nanabharana Bhushitam.
Pujayitva Bidhanena

Daridro Dhanaban Bhavet.

Iti Shri Kalidukkha Bimochan Tantre.
Dwadashapatale Shri Sheetala
Kabacham Sampurnam.

Om Hreem Shreem Hroom
Hraim Hroum Hrah.
Om Kharasthang Digambaram
Bikatanayanang Toyasthitang
Bhajami Swaha.
Swachchhandang
Prachandarupang
Namami Ambibhutoye.

Iti Shri Sheetala Kabacham
Sampurnam

Sheetala Chalisa

Doha

Joy Joy Joy Sheetala
Mata Jagatamoyi
Daser Dukhhharini
Doyamoyi Janani

Chalisa

Joy Sheetala Mata
Jagate Taba Stuti
Byadhinashini Devi
Tribhuvan Pujya Huti
Haste Marjani Dharane
Kulashe Pabitra Jal
Rog Byadhi Nash Karo
Dur Karo Sab Kal
Rasabhe Arudha Tumi
Digambari Rup
Darshanete Pap Nashe
Kate Dukkher Sup
Nimpata Ati Priya
Bhog Lagi Dhyan

Rishi Muni Yagye Tomar
Koren Ahvan
Ghor Ghor Pujita Tumi
Narnarir Pran
Shishur Byadhi Nash Koro
Dao Sukha Jiban
Je Jon Shraddhabhore
Kore Taba Bandana
Tar Ghore Sada Thake
Shanti Ar Dhan Dhona
Tumi Bishwambhara Mata
Karuna Koro Dase
Durdasha Nash Koro Ma
Rakha Sarbakale
Je Jon Sheetala Chalisa
Shraddhaya Japa Kore
Byadhi Byadha Dur Hoy
Sukha Samriddhi Ghore
Mata Tomar Prasadete
Dukkha Nash Pay
Sharanagata Jon Sokol
Siddhilabh Kore

Doha

Sheetala Mata Kripa Koro
Rakha Sabe Subhay
Jagate Sukha Shanti Dao
Daser Dukkha Jay

---

8) Nibedan Naivedya (Agnibihin)

- Offer **rice, yesterday's bread/ flatbread (roti) or pitha, jaggery, fruits, neem leaves, and cold milk or curd**.
- Sprinkle a little water to complete the offering.
- Using a **marjani (ritual whisk)**, symbolically express the intention of **warding off disease**.

9) Arati Pradakshin (without lamp)

- Perform Arati using flowers, a chamara (ritual whisk), or a mirror.• You may ring a bell.

Sheetala Arati

Om Joy Joy Sheetala May
Rasababahini Sheetala May
Marjani Haste Karunamoyi
Jwararogaharini May
Dugga Rupe Tumi Janani
Karuna Koro Sharanagatajoni
Bishphot Jwar Sab Byadhihara
Tumi Bishwamangala May
Nimpata Tomar Priya
Sheetalasnehe Sokol Hiya
Shishudaittyabhoy Nash Koro
Bhaktarakkha Koro May
Shubhra Barna Sheetala Mata
Sokol Dukkha Mochon Data
Ashirbade Purna Hok Pran
Tab Charone Namo Namah May
Arati Tomari Gai
Sheetala Janani Doyamoyi
Sharanagatarakkha Koro
Joy Joy Sheetala May

Sheetala Kirtan

Om Sheetalayai Namah
Sheetala Devi Namah

1. Mangalacharan

Om Shri Sheetala Devi Joy
Rasababahini Janani Joy
Namo Namo Shwetabastradharini
Jwararogabinashini May

2. Stab Kirtan Shuru

Sheetala Mayer Arati Gai
Karunamoyi Janani Mai
Nimpata Hate Shubhrabati
Shishu Byadhi Nasho Bhai
Shubhrangi Shashimukhi Devi
Shishur Dukkhahara Tumi
Bishphotak Peera Nash Koro
Dakshinyarupe Raksha Koro
Tumi Jananir Rupe Jago
Gramraksha Koro Diba Rat
Bhaktajaner Dake Chhute Aso

Mangal Koro Sokol Jat
He Sheetala Mata Shantir Data
Jwararog Peera Nash Koro
Santan Rakho Sustha Sukhe
Amra Sharanagata Raksha Koro
Nimer Chhayay Koro Biraj
Shwetapadme Tomar Saj
Marjani Hate Shweta Sharire
Tomari Kripay Kale Raksha
Joy Joy Sheetala Ma
Joy Joy Doyamoyi
Charone Sharan Loi Ma
Rakha Sarbada Sustha Hoi
Bhakter Dukkha Dur Koro Ma
Shishur Chokhe Hasi Dao
Tomar Charone Natashire
Sheetala Mayer Joy Joy Gao

10.Bishes Prarthana

(for Santan health)

Om Shri Sheetala Devyai Namah
Balakanang Sukshma
Rakshanam Kuru

11. Bisarjan Shanti O Phalshruti

Om Shri Sheetala Devyai Namah
Shri Matrinamah
Shantih Shantih Shantih

Sheetala Bisarjan Mantra

Om Sheetale Devi
Jatrakale Agaman Korilen
Ekhon Bisarjan Grahan Koro
Bhakter Basona Purna Koro
Raksha Koro Kripa Koro

Om Sheetale Namah
Om Bisarjayami

(After reciting the mantra, offer water or unbroken rice three times.)

12.Prasad Bitoro (Distribution)

- Give **rice, pitha, jaggery, and fruits** to family members and children.

Sahaj Mantrasamuha

Om Sheetalayai Namah
Om Shri Sheetala Devyai Namah
Om Hreem Shreem Sheetalayai Namah

Om Shri Sheetala Devyai Namah
Shri Matrinamah
Shantih Shantih Shantih

Additional Instructions and Variations

1. **Time:** Best performed at dawn or before sunrise.
2. **Fireless observance:** No cooking on fire; it is preferable to avoid lamps and incense. 3.**Who performs it:** Elder women of the family, the lady of the house, or a priest.

4. **Fasting:** Many families do not take freshly cooked food; only food prepared the previous day is consumed.

5. **Neem and cool water:** Symbolic of cooling and disinfecting qualities.

6. **For the sick:** In many households, neem leaves are placed near the patient's bed;

7. **Group worship:** One person recites while leading the others.

Practical Advice

- *If there is an infection, follow medical advice.*
- *Avoid smoke or strong fragrances around children.*
- *The worship is considered most auspicious when performed in accordance with the family's traditions.The worship is intended to inspire hope, strengthen faith, and cultivate inner strength.(this is not a substitute for medical treatment—consulting a doctor is essential).*

9 789356 552647

Printed at Repro India Ltd.